FUSE GLASS MAKING FOR BEGINNERS

Complete step by step guide for beginner's on how to use microwave kiln to make beautiful fused glass pendant at home

Lillian Jacobs

copyright@2021

Table of content

Chapter one

   Introduction

Chapter two

   Instructions and guide

Chapter three

   Stage 2: Safety First Kids....

Chapter four

   Stage 4: The Kiln Paper...

Chapter five

   Stage 5: Cutting the Glass...

   Stage 6: Breaking the Glass...

   Stage 7: Placing Your Glass...

   Stage 9: Time to Fire This Baby Up....

Chapter seven

   Stage 10: You See the Glow Then You Know....

Chapter eight

   Stage 12: And Now You Wait...

   Stage 13: So This Is Our Finished Product...

Chapter nine

Stage 14: Finishing the Piece...

Stage 15: Making It Into a Piece of Jewelry....

Chapter ten

Stage 17: Some Finished Pieces and How They Came to Be....

Chapter one

Introduction

Fused glass pendant is a beautiful piece of art that is made using a microwave kiln technique used to merge glass pieces together by incompletely melting the glass at high temperature. The heating is usually done in an electric oven.But, in this guide, you would learn to fuse glass in a microwave kiln at your home and make a beautiful abstract design glass pendant.

Chapter two

Instructions and guide

When making Fused Glass Jewelry in a Microwave Kiln certain steps and caution are taken to enable d finish product to appear perfect

It is astonishing how a gift can transform you. I got a microwave kiln for Christmas and it has opened up a universe of making intriguing pieces

Stage 1: materials You Will Need...

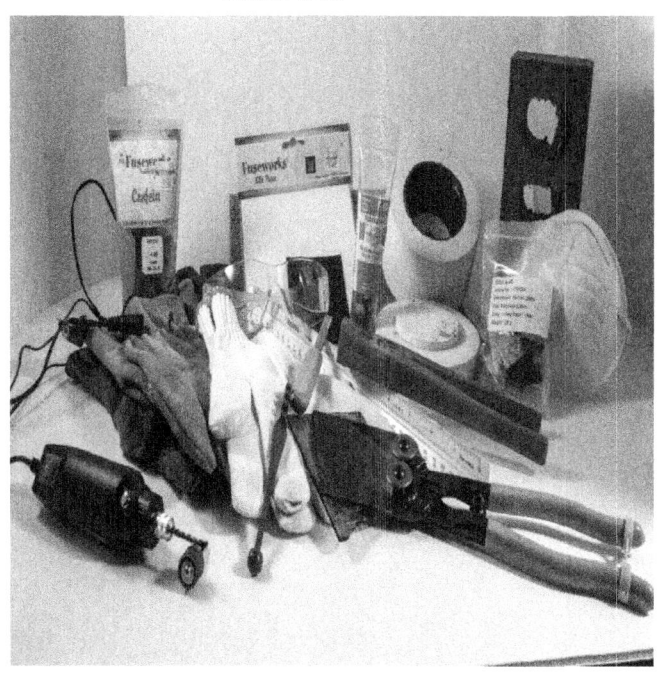

Alright, before you log off and run shouting seeing this picture, this is a combination of things you could require for this task. A portion of the things are need to haves. This Instrubctable depends on the little Fuseworks microwave oven. We'll separate it as we come. Don't be afriad. View at it as a fun experience through the glass.

Chapter three

Stage 2: Safety First Kids....

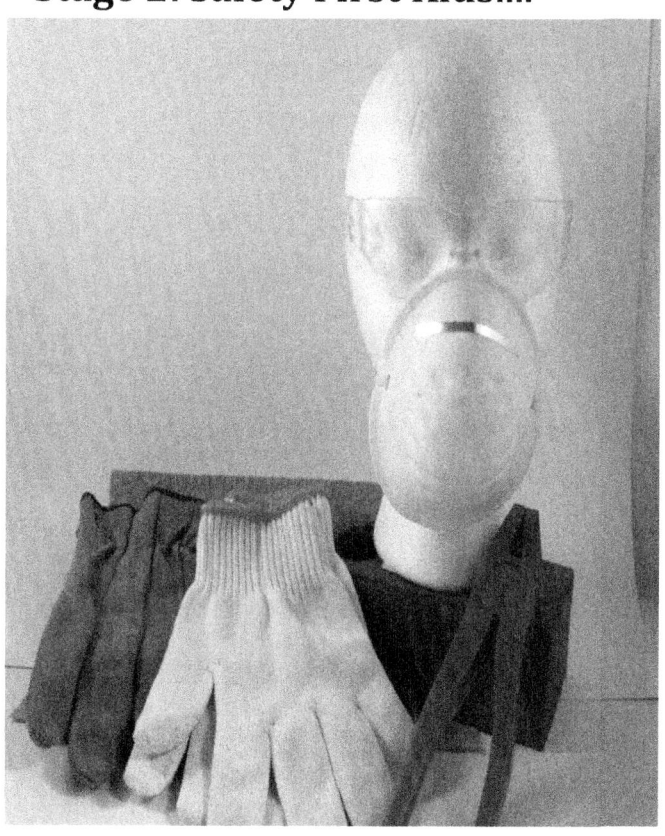

you are working with glass and hot temperatures. Security is an unquestionable requirement.

Protection for your eyes, lungs, and skin is of most extreme importance. Thus, don't take easy routes. Simply don't !!!

- Sturdy gloves will ensure your hands when breaking the glass.

- Heat Proof Gloves-They are for handling the kiln after heating and to remove the piece from the oven.

- Glass Pliers - For breaking glass.

- Dust Mask - So you don't get glass in your mouth, nose and lungs

- Safety Glasses - For breaking glass and use with the drill to complete your venture.

- A Heat safe surface - To sit the kiln on after the heating process.

Stage 3: What You Need for the Creation..

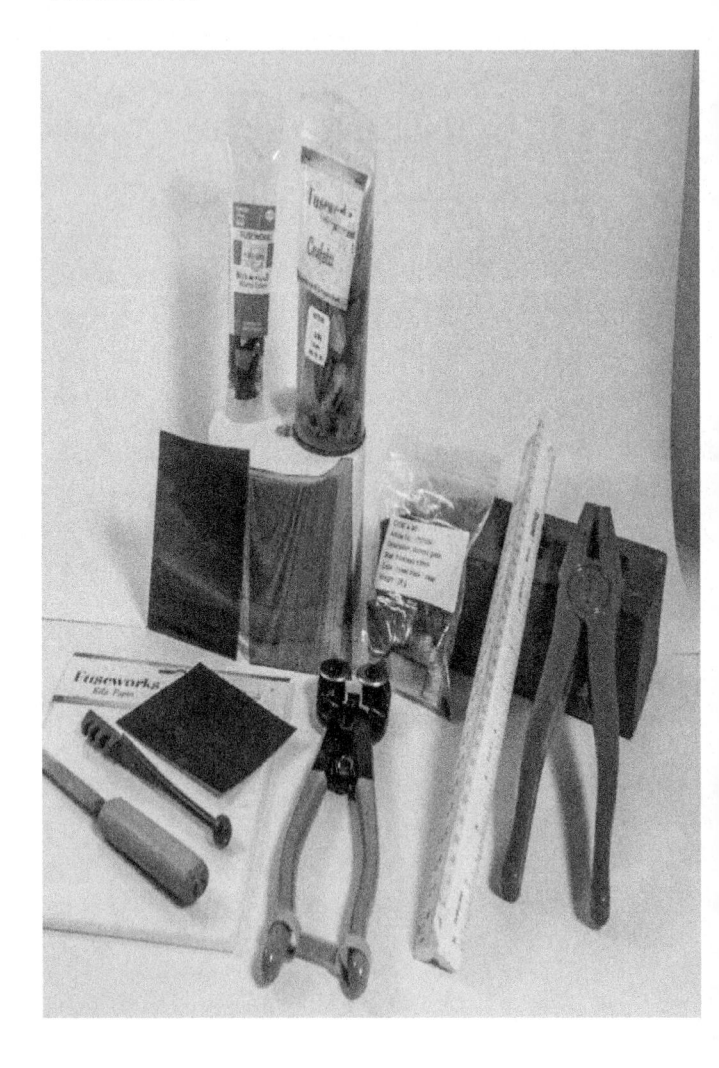

A portion of the things you should have are:

- THE KILN (clearly)
- Kiln Paper
- A glass shaper

•glass COE90 is the thing that is for the most part utilized for these undertakings. We will likewise address a portion of the various sorts of glass later.

- A Straight Edge
- A File
- Glass Pliers

A few things you should add later

- Different kinds of glass

- Glass/Tile Nippers

- Sandpaper

- Rotary device (like a Dremel)

Chapter four

Stage 4: The Kiln Paper...

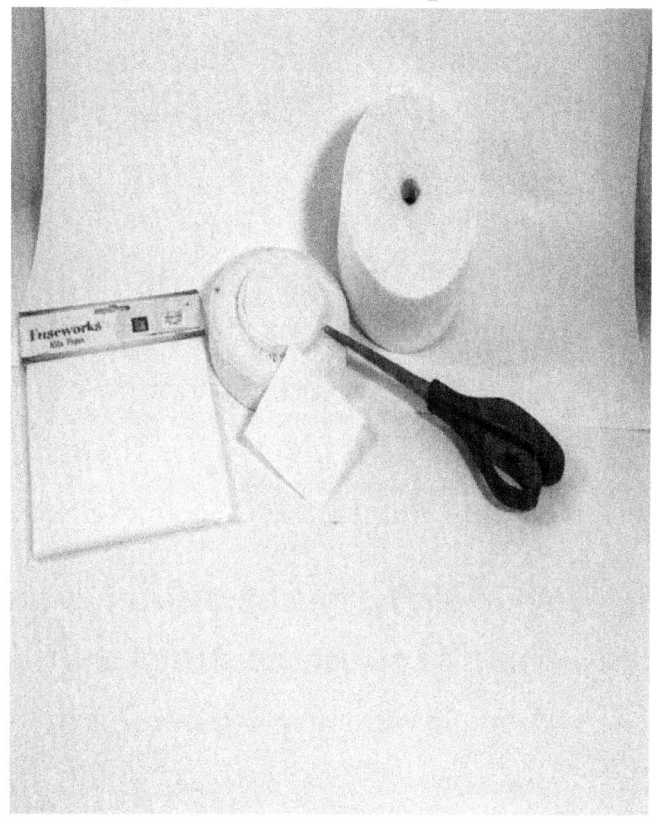

kiln paper should to be laid on the bed of the kiln each time you use it. The fuseworks paper I use, I can get four firings from each sheet. Sheet are 5/8" X 5/8". Just cut it into quarters when you get a piece of paper out of the bundle.

I for one decide to manage the paper into a round design close in size to the raised foundation of the kiln. That gives me a thought of the region I need to work with.

Additionally, ensure that the glass doesn't contact the side of the oven. It will stick and can harm your oven.

This paper is a one hit wonder. Kiln paper can't be reused. One use and throw it.

Chapter five

Stage 5: Cutting the Glass...

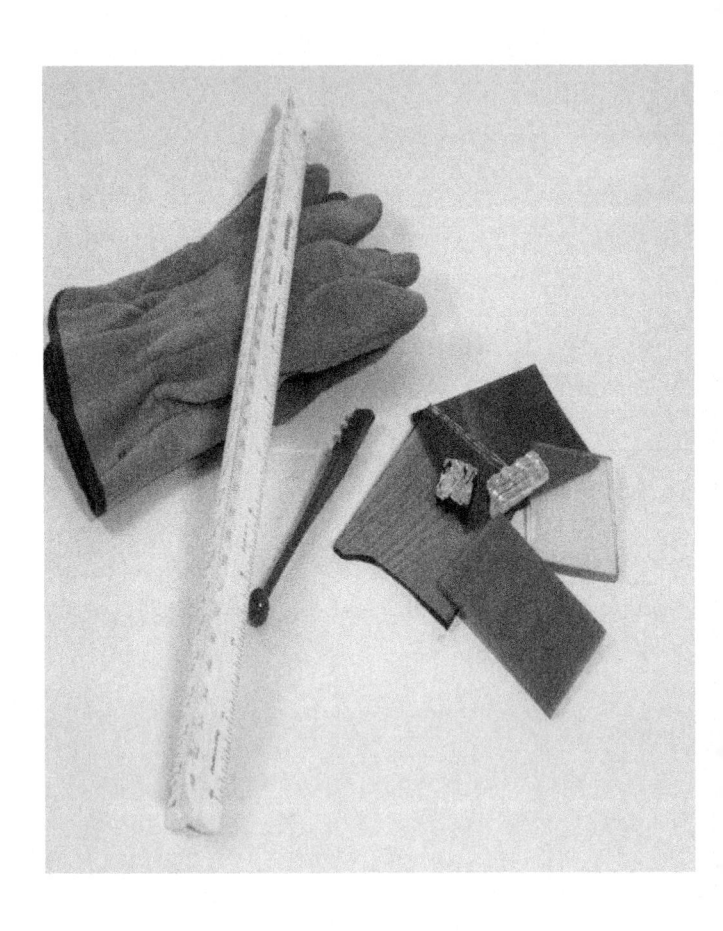

You won't slice totally through the glass, you are seriously scoring the glass. You are making a slight indention in the glass with the goal that you will actually want to see where the break will happen.

Use your straightedge and position it on the glass. At that point you take the glass shaper [cutter] and applying pressure, you go the length of the glass. This is will leave the score line as found in the last photograph.

This is the line that you will break.

Here is a little something that may be useful, you ought to hear the glass shaper[cutter] coming the outside of the glass. In case you do not hear it, you most likely need to apply more pressure.

Stage 6: Breaking the Glass...

I have utilized three distinct strategies to break the glass. Two were very successful, one not in the least.

Technique one..... Glass Pliers, they handle the glass solidly without gnawing into it. Extraordinary, this is the most ideal way.

Technique two... Until I got glass pincers, I utilized the edge of my kitchen ledge. It functioned admirably.

Technique three.... Utilizing standard family pincers. Don't, it will nibble into the glass.

After picking your technique, simply snap it rapidly, actually like ripping off a gauze, do what needs to be done.

Stage 7: Placing Your Glass...

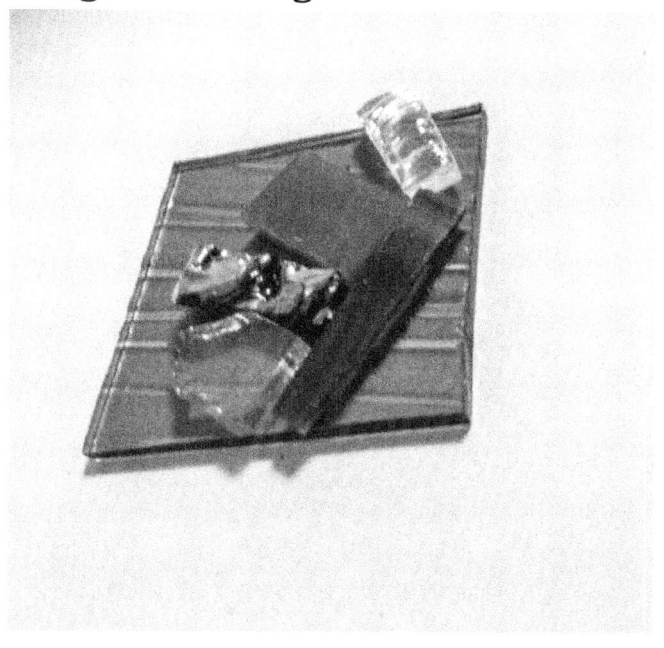

Whenever you have cut and broken the glass, then assemble your creation. For this Instructable, I picked six unique shades[colour] of glass. It is your proje ct, you may combine different colours. Simply play with it, have some good times. Simply appreciate the experience of making fuse glass.

Chapter six

Stage 8: Placing It in the Kiln....

This is pretty much simple. place the kiln paper, place your design on top and put the top on.
Indeed, ensure none of the glass is contacting the bed or the sides

of the oven. It isn't that I have done it or anything, we should simply say I know now not. Additionally, on the off chance that you think something moved when you put the top on, you can check it before you begin terminating. When you begin terminating, don't eliminate the top until the terminating interaction is finished.

Simply know that on the off chance that you do eliminate the top, you may need to realign the glass to get the impact you needed.

Stage 9: Time to Fire This Baby Up....

When you put the kiln into the microwave, you should sort out the best an ideal time for your microwave.

My microwave is 900 watts. Contingent upon the kind of glass I am melding, it typically fires in around 5 minutes to 5 minutes and 30 seconds.

Check the wattage on your microwave. It will fire quicker with a higher wattage.

Taking into account that seconds can matter. Being a dinosaur and having a dial microwave, I needed to exchange up. It is important, so you can get a modest one at the Walmart close to you.

Chapter seven

Stage 10: You See the Glow Then You Know....

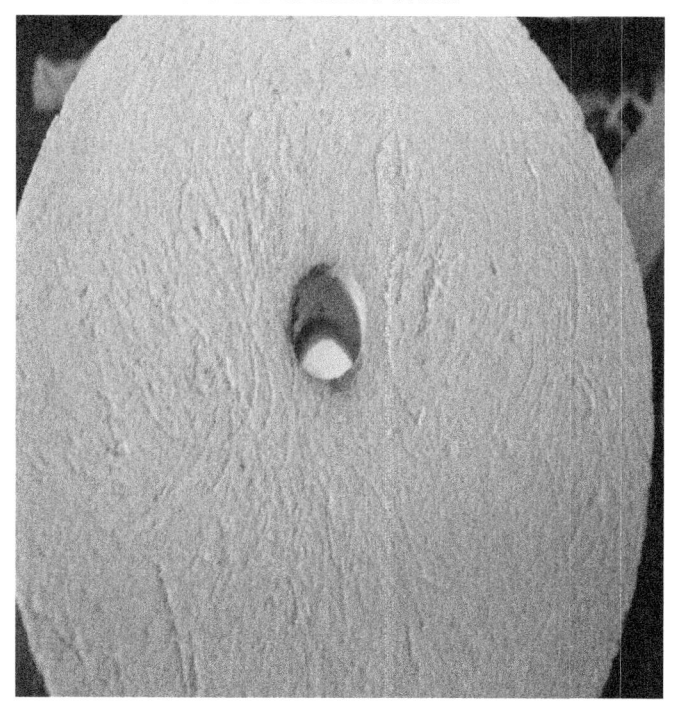

When the kiln is up to temperature, the middle opening in the highest point of the oven will gleam, that is the point at which you will realize that the terminating is going on. It is then that you eliminate the kiln from the microwave.

Stage 11: Glove Up....

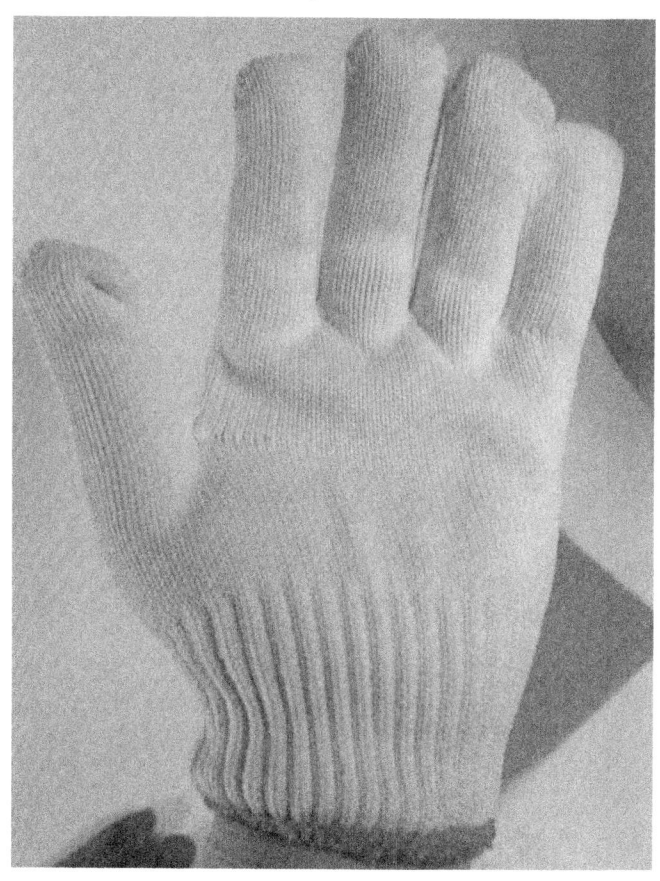

In any case, WAIT..... don't for any reason grab hold of the kiln with bare hands . Serious injury will most definitely happen. In the event that you are drawing near to the heating to end, glove up. You should wear gloves when dealing with the kiln and the completed piece after it sets.

Caution: Try not to hold on to it for long, albeit these gloves make moving the kiln endurable. It can in any case harm the gloves if you hold it excessively long. Same with the completed piece that emerges from the oven. At the point when you move, move with goal. Move the kiln to the heat safe surface (recollect my block). The equivalent applies to the completed piece. It is still hot.

Chapter eight
Stage 12: And Now You Wait...

The piece needs to sit in the oven for 30 minutes whenever it is remove from the microwave. This is to permit time for the glass to solidify and fuse together. This can be an exceptionally noisy cycle, so in the event that you hear something that sound awful coming from inside the oven, endure it, don't lift the cover until the full 30 minutes lapses. I normally go get another thing to do while waiting. To a few of us, 30 minutes seems like until the end of time. In the event that you accomplish something different, your view of time is modified and the time has passed before you know it.

Whenever you have taken out the lid from the oven and spot the highest point of the oven with the little opening down on a warmth safe surface, it needs to cool, it has held sufficient warmth to take a strong, separating it into a magma like puddle and permitted it to turn into a strong again so it needs to cool. Try not to utilize it again until it is cool to the touch. Leave the base setting on the block. It is fine where it is.

Stage 13: So This Is Our Finished Product...

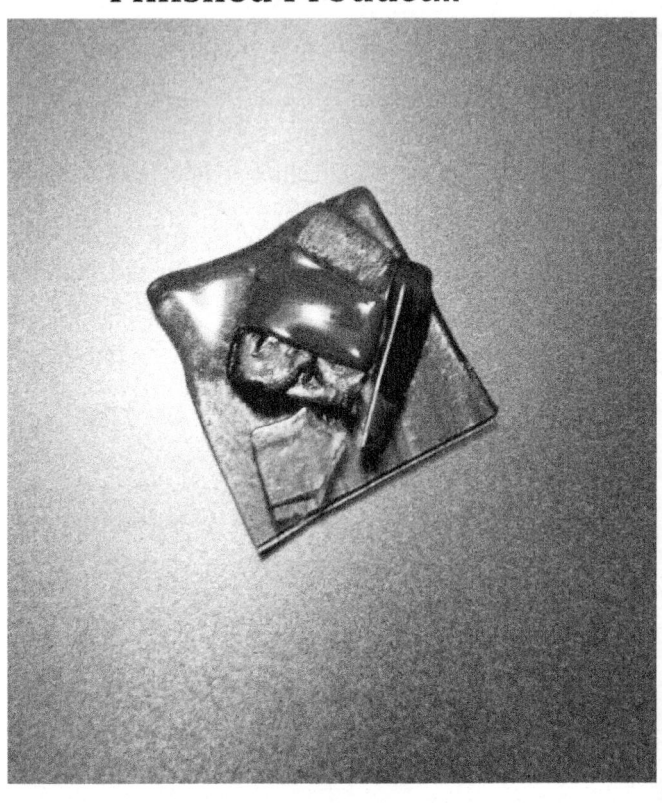

You saw these similar pieces before in this Instructable. I really made this piece just for this venture. There were a few errors, that will occur. In some cases, it doesn't heat uniformly and you can see it in the completed venture. You have two options here, figure out how to adore the blemishes or you can attempt to fire it once more. Simply make sure to utilize new kiln paper and once in a while completing the piece again functions admirably, here and there it doesn't.

Chapter nine

Stage 14: Finishing the Piece...

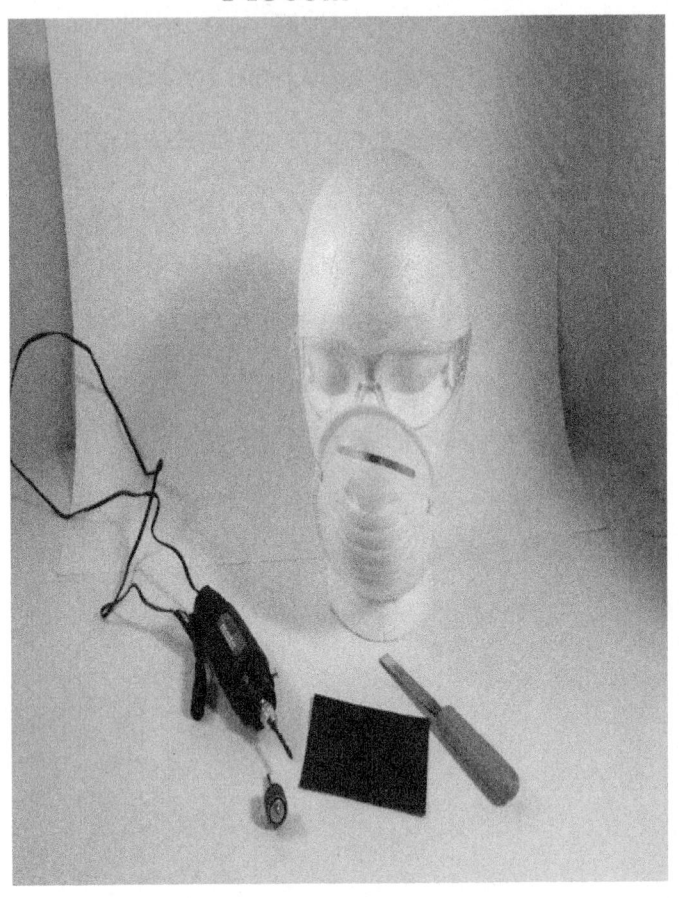

Utilize your file, sand paper or rotary tool to smooth any rough edges left This will make your piece a smooth completed, pleasantly cleaned pendant. Make sure to utilize safety glass and your particle mask.

Stage 15: Making It Into a Piece of Jewelry....

You can make a pendant, a ring, an arm band[bracelet] or earring. It is totally up to you. Make what you need, make what you love, simply make.

E6000 turns out extraordinary for following the completed piece to the clear or finding that you pick.

Stage 16: Some Terms You Might Here...

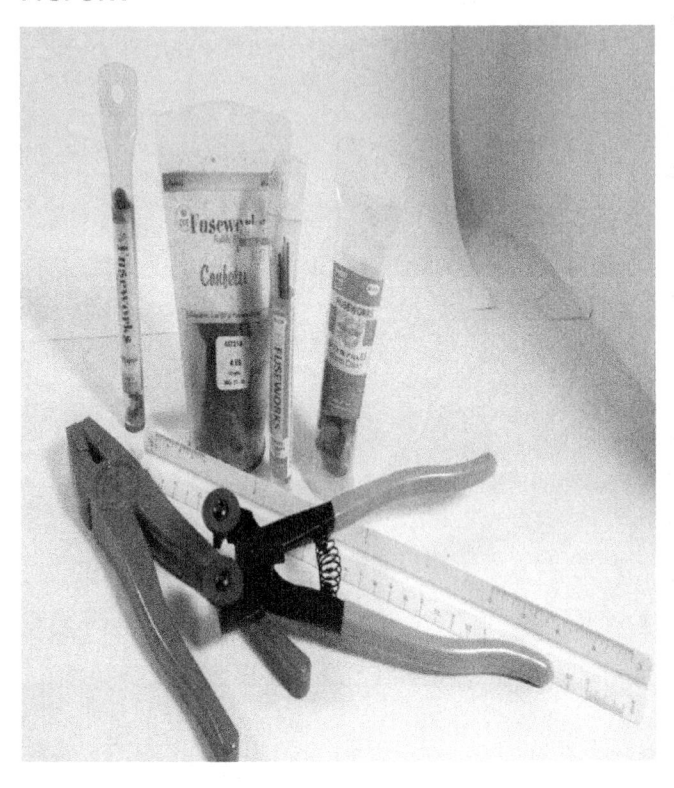

Frit, Bits and Piece or Confetti - These are simply little bits of glass that can be utilized in your piece. It isn't the level pieces you would normally use for the base of your piece.

Millefiori - Oxford word reference characterizes this as "a sort of elaborate glass where various glass bars of various sizes and shadings are melded and cut into areas that structure different examples, normally inserted in vapid straightforward glass to make things like paperweights." Now, making an interpretation of that into plain talk, it is little, lumps of glass with various tones that have been combined by the organization that makes it to give you a truly cool impact with not as much exertion. It is quite magnificent stuff.

Dichoric glass-This implies two tones. A portion of the dichroics you purchase might be brilliant in nature others may have a more metallic look. It is AMAZING for that BAM piece essentially in light of the fact that it is receptive to light.

Stringers: This is little poles of a solitary tone, that can be effectively penniless to add as a filler for you piece.

Youngsters - Nippers are utilized for tile and glass. They can give you to a greater degree a cut than a straight cut from the glass shaper.

Glass Pliers - These can be bought at some tool shops or Hobby Lobby conveys them.

Chapter ten

Stage 17: Some Finished Pieces and How They Came to Be....

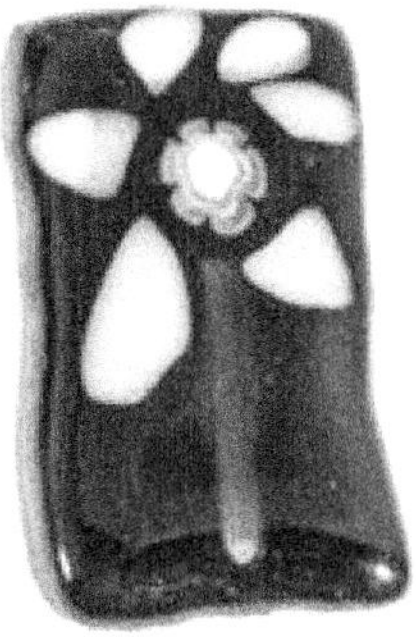

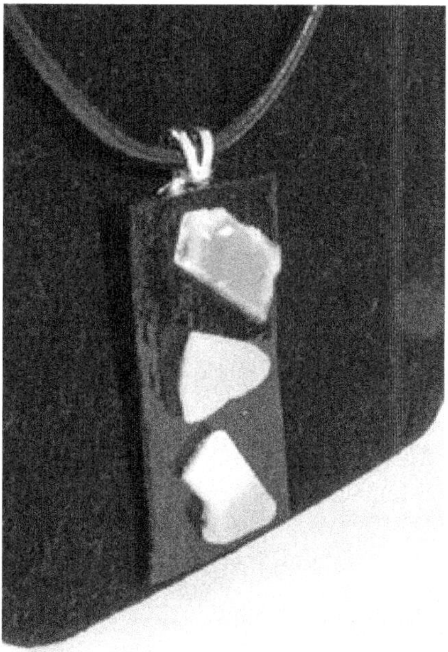

The first you see is a bigger part of dichroic glass. I added some dim hued stringers to give it some definition. This piece is smooth.

The subsequent one, the middle is millefiori, white shards I cut with youngsters and the stem of the blossom, well that is a stringer. This piece additionally has a smooth completion.

The third one, a companion has named the Sushi accessory, it has a dark base and it is finished because of a more limited terminating time.

The last piece, is red frit with a solitary piece of white frit in the middle. The leaves were cut with youngsters. This piece is additionally finished.

Expectation you delighted in the excursion. Expectation you picked up something. Expectation you attempt it. Simply make sure to unwind and play around with it. It is simply glass, magma and glass once more.

Stage 18: Once Last Thing Before I Go....

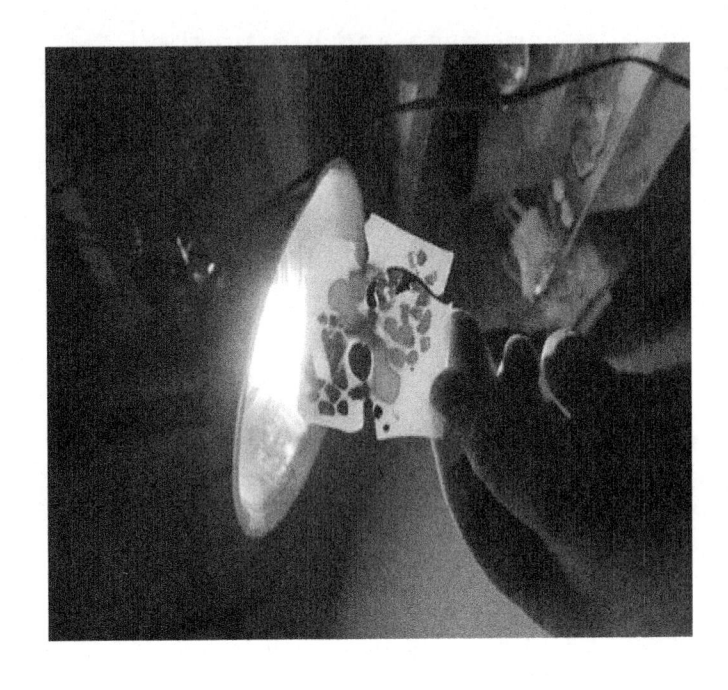

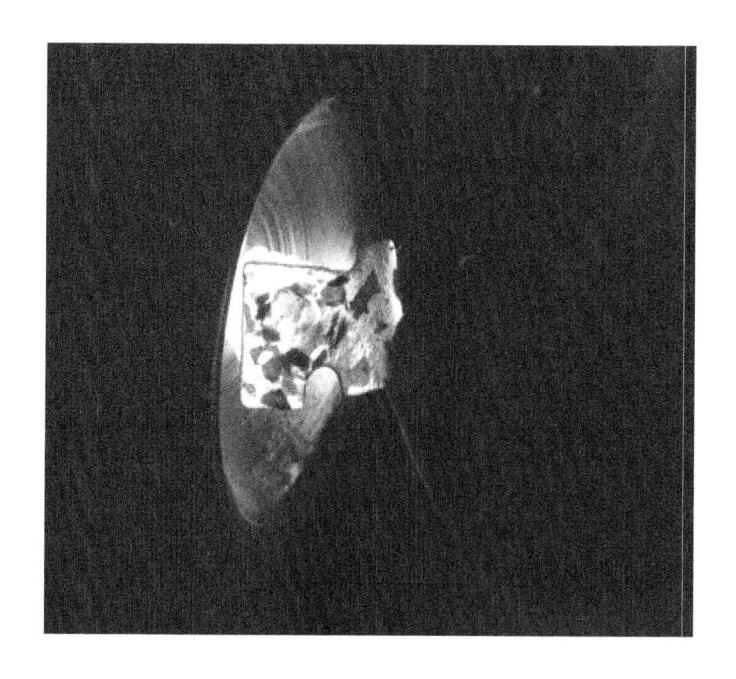

Those pieces that do end up so perfectly, those can be pretty freakin' cool also, simply place them before a LED light and lookout them light up, at that point judge them.

NOW...Go have some good times, yet be protected.

Printed in Great Britain
by Amazon